ForensicsNation Bushwhacker Program

©2012 Dr. Leland Benton

"Any sufficiently advanced technology is indistinguishable from magic."

- Arthur C. Clarke

Introduction

Welcome to ForensicsNation. I'm Dr. Leland Benton and I am the Chief Forensics Investigator for ForensicsNation. My company – Neternatives.com – is actually made up of 32-divisons with ForensicsNation being the largest. As the Managing Director of Neternatives, I wear many hats but the one that keeps me the most active is forensics. I am the public voice or mouthpiece for the company. Because of the nature of our business, our forensic investigators remain behind a screen of anonymity. We work mostly out of a series of control rooms. Our computer systems are second to none and we track cyber-crime worldwide.

I create the software programs that catch bad guys. I also create the methods and modalities ForensicsNation uses to identify the bad guys and compile evidence against them.

Forensics, by definition, is the identification of the perpetrators of crime and the compilation of evidence against them. We aren't some cyber-NCIS or Dog the Bounty Hunter nor do we have any police authority to arrest the criminals that we find. Our job is to find them, compile the evidence against them and then turn it over to law enforcement or whomever has hired us such as large corporations, individuals, bounty hunters, bail bondsmen, etc.

The ForensicsNation Bushwhacker Program is like nothing you have ever seen before. You may be selling a Clickbank diet program online and making a $50 commission and that's okay. I catch bad guys and collect very large rewards and once you learn my trade you will see just how profitable it is and can be for you. Where to you find perpetrators with rewards on their heads?

Here's one site and there are hundreds of sites like this that we identify for you in our program:

http://www.mostwantedhoes.com/rewards/

The ForensicsNation Bushwhacker Program is made up of two parts.

The ForensicsNation Bushwhacker Program teaches you how to protect yourself and your loved ones from cyber attacks, identity theft, hacking, and more.

You are also taught to basically become an amateur Internet sleuth. We will supply you with the tools; most of them are free and some you have to pay for and we also provide you with a checklist where you can offer your services to small local businesses and individual to protect them from cyber attacks too.

So, just how vulnerable are YOU? I am going to demonstrate your cyber-vulnerability but I am warning you in advance that this is happening every day!

Your websites – most of you reading this own Wordpress blogs. It takes less than 30-seconds to break into a blog's WP Admin area using a free software program available on torrent sites. I will show you a four-digit code to add to your blog's username that will prevent any bad guy breaking into your admin area and wreaking havoc before you even know you have been penetrated. BTW – I caught one clever bad guy who broke into an admin area of a very big online marketer and changed the PayPal account username directing all of the sales to his PayPal account. By the time this was discovered he had made off with over $250,000 in sales. Yes, we tracked him down and he was prosecuted and most of the money was recovered but not all of it.

Your personal information – with our company's proprietary software, it takes me all of 10-minutes to compile a dossier on you complete with all of your bank accounts, investment accounts, driver's license, social security number, personal information such as family members, their names and personal info, property records, cars you own, and much more. In fact, the amount of information I can compile on you is almost endless and it is your fault because you placed this information or allowed it to be placed on the Internet without even realizing how vulnerable it makes you. I will show you how to protect your identity and literally drop off the grid. In conjunction with one of our sister divisions – PrivacyNations – I will also show you how to make your information inaccessible.

Your location – if you carry a cell phone, a driver's license or use your car, I know where you are and where you have been 24/7. Every cell phone has a GPS tracking chip in it (not just the smart phones; the analog phones too), every driver's license now has a RFID chip in it that works off the cell phone antennas, and the new cars have GPS locators in them like the GM OnStar. You can remove the battery from your cell phone to disable the GPS function but there is nothing you can do about your driver's license.

If you are an online marketer dealing in mobile commerce, you have probably heard of a GPS Fence. You can "tag" a business with a GPS tag and when any of the business owner's customers comes within 300-yards of the business, a text message is triggered to the customer's cell phone. In forensics, we have what is called GPS Laser tagging where I can place a tag on any physical object and track it by satellite through one of our divisions – TheoSat – so there is nowhere to hide, people! How do you think the feds catch bad guys so quickly? Now the really tech savvy bad guys know all of what I have just taught you and more and they know how to protect themselves but everybody slips up and when they do I own them!

Your physical well-being - GPS is a good thing when used properly. One of our divisions – PinpointProtect - offers GPS protection services to high profile people, people who travel extensively, women, children, and anyone vulnerable to physical attack or abduction. Each person is given a tracker to carry and the tracker has an SOS button so when they get into trouble they can just push the SOS button. Our control room tracks them and then provides whatever services are required to assist the person. Each person is also given an Internet Interface where they can dial in and see where they are 24/7. If they get lost, they can easily find out there location and how to get to where they are supposed to be. They can give their login coordinates to anyone they choose – wife, parents, etc – and these people can login and find out where they are 24/7. Yes, GPS does have its useful purposes. One customer of ours is a game hunter and he got lost in Alaska. He hit the SOS button and he was rescued within 2-hours.

And it is not just individuals that are vulnerable. You all have heard of the hacking group "Anonymous" that hacked the financial institutions that refused to do business with Wikileaks. This same group threatened the Mexican Drug Cartels when the cartels captured one of their members. DUMB...real dumb! I do TV, radio and magazine interviews weekly. I was asked to comment on Anonymous going after the Mexican Drug Cartels. Here is the article. Slide down the page; my comment was quite short:

http://www.dailydot.com/news/anonymous-mexico-opcorrupcion/

There is a good deal of stuff to get to in The ForensicsNation Bushwhacker Program so be prepared to study. This guidebook will cover computer investigation, Internet investigation, and Internet forensics. I have left all of the resources from the first program intact because you will need them. I have added some resources that were not available to the first program users. At the very end of this guidebook, I have included a Bonus Section. I have taken information from our sister division – PrivacyNations.com – and included it since their programs and products are highly synergistic with ForensicsNation and you will undoubtedly be incorporating its product lines into your services...enjoy!

We are going to be talking in the context of running an Internet investigation and forensics business. I am going to outline for you what is needed and as we go along this will give you the ability to compile a checklist.

There are many aspects to this business. You may incorporate all of them or pick and choose the ones that best suit your talents and passions. I don't expect you to turn it into a behemoth that ForensicsNation has become but it certainly possible and the market demand for what we do is growing faster than we can provide services. But note, a good many aspects of this business will not become available to you without the proper training so pay close attention to the Continuing Education and Certification section below.

We are going to discuss business structure, licensing, insurance, continuing education, certification, and marketing throughout this course and a bunch of other stuff too. Please do not cut any corners; everything I discuss is essential in protecting you and your business as well as maximizing the profit potential.

Business Structure

The way you structure your forensics business is important. Do not operate as a sole proprietor. The best way is a limited liability corporation (LLC) and the best place to incorporate is Nevada.

Please be sure to consult an attorney. You will need an attorney to assist you in issuing subpoenas, and you will also need an attorney specializing in Federal law too. I would pay close attention to selecting an attorney and get their fee schedule up front. They will be a big part of your business so the attorney's availability is important. Ask questions! Can his paralegal prepare and issue subpoenas? Once you begin operations, you will identify other legal needs as well.

In the Bonus Section, there is more information on Nevada LLCs.

Insurance

A good insurance agent will advise you on the appropriate coverages. Be sure to make it known to your insurance agent that you ARE NOT a field investigator and the majority of your work will be from your home/office on your computer.

You will need a very good general liability policy with $1-million in coverage and if you can qualify for it, you will also need a $5-million Umbrella Policy.

Don't forget to insurance all of your equipment and computer plus all of your software too.

Products & Services

Here is a partial list of products and services you can provide:

Computer/Internet Forensics

Data Recovery
Internet Fraud Investigations
Other Computer Related Crimes
Theft of Trade Secrets or Intellectual Property
Internet Related Fraud
Theft of Trade Secrets
Criminal Activities
Hacking
Theft
Fraud
Forensic Computer Examinations
Computer Data Forensic Analysis
Lost Data Recovery
Hidden Data Recovery
"Exact" Copies of Hard Disks and Computer Media
Unlocking Passwords and Lost Password Recovery

Digital Discovery for Law Firms and Litigation
Data Authentication
Data Format Conversion
"Suspect Employee" Internal Corporate Inquiries
"Trojan Horse" Hijacked Computer Analysis
Deleted E-mail and Instant Message Chat recovery
Kazaa/Morpheus/Grokster (etc.) file sharing analysis
ICQ / AOL Instant Message / Yahoo / MSN6 and similar instant message chat recovery and analysis
Internet History and Web Surfing Activity Analysis
Data Recovery from Damaged Floppies and CD-Rs
Wipe ("sterilize") old hard drives to DOD Standards
Computer Registry Analysis

Internet Investigations

Email Tracing
Email search
Finding people
Background check
Address search
Public record search
Criminal record search
DMV record check
Court record search
Adoptee search
Birth mother search
Property record search
Death records search
Employee Internet Abuse
Pornography and Child Pornography Issues
Identity Theft Investigations
Suspected Spousal Infidelity
Network or System Intrusion Detection
Internet or Email Harassment Cases
Nigerian (419) Scams
Spousal Infidelity Issues
Corporate Due Diligence
Jury Member Screening
Asset Searches
Intellectual Property Issues
Missing Person Locates
Internet Expert Witness Services
Internet Defamation
Stalking
Incident Response
Litigation Support

Website tracing

Computer Investigation

Keystroke logging - (often called keylogging) is the action of tracking (or logging) the keys struck on a keyboard, typically in a covert manner so that the person using the keyboard is unaware that their actions are being monitored. There are numerous keylogging methods, ranging from hardware and software-based approaches to electromagnetic and acoustic analysis.

Counter forensics - (sometimes counter forensics) is a general term for a set of techniques used as countermeasures to forensic analysis.

Cryptanalysis - where it is obvious that intercepted data contains a message (though that message is encrypted)

Data remanence - is the residual representation of data that remains even after attempts have been made to remove or erase the data.

Disk encryption - uses disk encryption software or hardware to encrypt every bit of data that goes on a disk or disk volume. Disk encryption prevents unauthorized access to data storage. The term "full disk encryption" (or whole disk encryption) is often used to signify that everything on a disk is encrypted, including the programs that can encrypt bootable operating system partitions. But they must still leave the master boot record (MBR), and thus part of the disk, unencrypted. There are, however, hardware-based full disk encryption systems that can truly encrypt the entire boot disk, including the MBR.

Encryption - is the process of transforming information (referred to as plaintext) using an algorithm (called a cipher) to make it unreadable to anyone except those possessing special knowledge, usually referred to as a key.

Hidden file and hidden directory - a hidden directory or hidden file on a computer is a directory (folder) or file which a user cannot see by default. Hidden directories most often serve to hide important operating system-related files and user preferences. However, malicious programs can also use this functionality to hide their presence from unaware users.

Information technology audit - An information technology audit, or information systems audit, is an examination of the management controls within an Information technology (IT) infrastructure. The evaluation of obtained evidence determines if the information systems are safeguarding assets, maintaining data integrity, and operating effectively to achieve the organization's goals or objectives. These reviews may be performed in conjunction with a financial statement audit, internal audit, or other form of attestation engagement.

Steganalysis - The goal of steganalysis is to identify suspected packages, determine whether or not they have a payload encoded into them, and, if possible, recover that payload.

Pricing

Pricing varies by location and competition. On the forensics side, there is virtually no competition. My people bill out at $250/hour - $350/hour for forensics. When we do a business analysis and protect their computers, we charge a flat fee of $25/computer.

Fees are normally based upon an hourly rate of $250 to $350 per hour, depending upon the operating system, the difficulty of the examination or recovery, and whether court testimony may be necessary. This rate should be determined and quoted before any limited or complete examination begins.

Four types of examinations: (1) a <u>preliminary evaluation</u> for $600 to determine whether further examination is advisable, (2) an intermediate, <u>limited examination</u> of 10 to 20 hours for finding specific items of interest to the client (the time may increase or decrease based on the operating system, hardware difficulties encountered, multiple hard drives encountered, the number of floppies or other media to be examined, password or encryption problems to be resolved, the type of data encountered, or other specific examination requirements made by the client), (3) a <u>complete examination</u> of up to 35 billable hours (which may increase or decrease for reasons similar to those mentioned above), and (4) a <u>complete data audit/digital autopsy</u> of the hard drive or other media. (A complete data audit or digital autopsy identifies and catalogs every existing type of data on a hard disk drive and presents a detailed and exhaustive report to the client or to the courts.)

Retainer: A retainer of 50% of the estimated examination cost is required before the limited or complete examination is started. A signed retention agreement is required before conducting an examination. The retention agreement specifies the scope and details of the examination to be performed.

Travel rates: Our out-of-town daily rate is 2 times the quoted hourly rate, plus reasonable per diem and expenses. The in-town travel rate is 1/2 the quoted hourly rate.

In the past, Computer Forensic Examinations could run tens of thousands of dollars because of the manpower necessary to thoroughly examine a hard-drive. With the advancement of technology in the Computer Forensics arena that is no longer the case. The software and hardware available now make the price of Computer Forensics affordable and well worth the investment. The prices can range from $250/hour to $350/hour and the process involves basically three steps: Acquisition, Investigation, and Reporting. Acquisitions usually cost less than $500.00. Investigation and Reporting, of course, depend on the nature of your case. In most instances, searching and reporting can be completed in less than 15 hours and the total analysis is usually less than $4500.00.

Licensing

I know of no particular licensing requirements but to be safe check with your state and local authorities. You are not a field investigator nor are you a bounty hunter. You will work with these people but you do not have any contact with perpetrators with the exception of going to court to testify. If you seriously apply yourself to this business and garner the necessary certifications as listed in the Education section, then you will qualify as an expert witness and the fees are enormous. I charge $500/hour to testify in court.

Continuing Education & Certification

There is no silver-bullet certification available for forensic investigators, but apart from the Certified Information Systems Security Professional (CISSP) there are a few other diverse, vendor-neutral certifications for those who wish to establish and enhance their skill sets.

Certified Information Forensics Investigator (CIFI) - Offered by the International Information Systems Forensics Association, CIFI is designed to demonstrate expertise in all aspects of the information investigative process.
http://www.infoforensics.org

Certified Forensic Computer Examiner (CFCE) and Certified Electronic Evidence Collection Specialist (CEECS) - Offered by the International Association of Computer Investigative Specialists. CFCE and CEECS are forensic certifications offered for law enforcement officers. http://www.cops.org/cfce.htm

GIAC Certified Forensic Analyst (GCFA) - Offered by the SANS Institute's Global Information Assurance Certification group, GCFA tests the knowledge and skills to handle forensic scenarios, incident investigations, and forensic investigation of networks.
http://www.giac.org/certifications/security/gcfa.php

Advanced Information Security & Assurance (AIS) - Offered by the Security University, AIS is an eight-module certification focusing on distinct skill sets within computer security. Although the certification is not just for forensics there is a strong forensic component. http://www.securityuniversity.net

EnCE - The EnCase Certified Examiner Program offers certifications for those who have mastered their EnCase Guidance Software. Training courses and a copy of the software are required to gain the certification. This program is very reasonably priced at $200 for the exam (available through Prometric).
http://www.guidancesoftware.com/training/EnCE_certification.aspx

Computer Forensic External Certification (CCE) - Originally designed for law enforcement by the IACIS, this certification is now open to those with the experience and knowledge to complete the rigorous testing. The exam costs $750.
http://www.cops.org/External%20Certification.htm

Q/FE Qualified Forensics Expert - This less of a traditional certification than an in-depth training class with an exam and certificate at the end. The materials included will prepare you to find the cause of attack, compile evidence, and handle corporate repercussions. The cost of the course is US $2,995
http://www.securityuniversity.net/certification.htm

TruSecure ICSA Certified Security Associate - Although it is not directly a forensics certification, this overall security certification is highly respected and covers essential forensics procedures.
http://www.icsalabs.com/icsa/topic.php?tid=fdghgf54645-ojojoj567

CCE - Certified Computer Examiner - You'll get a full dose of the technical side of data recovery and handling, but this certification stresses the importance of "following sound evidence handling and storage procedures and following sound examination procedures". The exam is $395 and many self-study materials are available.
http://www.certified-computer-examiner.com/

Computer Forensic Training Online - Get online training and CCE certification through Kennesaw State University. The course fee is $2700.
http://www.kennesaw.edu/coned/sci/for_online.htm

Here are sites to checkout:

http://www.giac.org/certification/certified-forensic-analyst-gcfa
http://www.acfei.com/
http://www.infosecinstitute.com/courses/computer_forensics_training.html

Marketing

This is the fun part....marketing. I may wear a good many hats and have a good load of responsibilities but marketing means fun to me because it is the action that makes everything happen.

First of all, since forensics is an unusual business and thanks to television, it carries an enormous amount of public awareness and respect. When someone asks you what you do and you tell them you are an Internet Forensics Investigator, you can be sure a conversation will follow.

What this means is that the marketing side is easy and you are not considered another salesman or solicitor. Your profession demands respect!

Here is a partial list of your main customers:

Law Firms
Accountants, Fraud Examiners and Auditors
Businesses and Corporations
Law Enforcement, Police Agencies and Prosecutors
Courts and the Judiciary (as a neutral third-party expert to the Court or a Special Master)
Private Investigators
Insurance Companies
Victims of Computer Crimes or Torts
Students or others suffering data loss

It would be advisable to prepare a nice brochure with all of your services and contact information. The customers listed above always have more work than investigators so be prepared to get a high influx of business. Only list the services you are interested in doing. Unless you take some training courses, some of what is listed is out of your realm of expertise.

For esthetics purposes if for nothing else, it is important that you "look" the part. Go here for badges and certification wallets

http://www.collectiblebadges.com/category/1_badge_wallets_holders.htm

NOTE: UNDERSTAND YOU HAVE NO POLICE AUTHORITY AND ALL THIS DOES IS GIVE YOU A PROFESSIONAL LOOK. DO NOT USE THESE TO IMPERSONATE ANY PEACE OFFICE. THERE ARE HUGE PENALTIES FOR DOING SO!!!

Equipment

When it comes to amateur equipment Brickhouse Security is best. Checkout the following
Brickhouse Security - Our Proffered Provider of Quality Spy Gear
http://www.anrdoezrs.net/click-5444568-10683802

- **Audio Spy Equipment -** Audio voice analysis and modification spy equipment such as voice stress analyzers, voice changers and transformers for use with telephones and cell phones.
  http://www.spygear4u.com/voice-changers.asp?PARTNER=applied5564

- **Audio Amplifiers -** Sound amplification equipment for listening to people from a distance.
  http://www.einvestigator.com/spy_equipment/sound_amplifier.htm

- **Hidden Cameras -** Spy security camera equipment. Covert and easily concealed hidden security cameras, wireless security cameras, stealth cams for hats, camera glasses, hidden camera buttons, and more.
  http://www.tkqlhce.com/click-5444568-10676005

- **Computer Spy Gear -** Equipment for spying on computers, recording internet surfing activity, logging keystrokes, catching a cheating spouse.
  http://www.anrdoezrs.net/click-5444568-10943015

- **Hidden Safes -** hide your valuables in unexpected places. Diversion safes and unique home security products and other gear
  http://www.einvestigator.com/spy_equipment/hidden_diversion_safes.htm

- **Digital Voice Recorders / Audio Recorders -** Audio spy recording equipment including digital voice recorders, telephone recorders, and tape recorders are useful for taking witness statements, recording notes about a case and more.
  http://www.einvestigator.com/spy_equipment/digital_audio_voice_recorders.htm

- **Electronic Bug Detectors -** Electronic bug detection devices are useful for performing basic countermeasure checks either for your home security or as a security service to your clients. Electronic bug detectors help detect and locate all major types of electronic surveillance devices including room, phone, body bugs, microphones, video transmitters, and tape recorders.
  http://www.spygear4u.com/bug-detection-devices.asp?PARTNER=applied5564

- **GPS Tracking Devices -** Covert GPS vehicle tracking devices for monitoring the travel activities of company, fleet and private vehicles.
  http://www.anrdoezrs.net/click-5444568-10655533

- **Listening Devices** - Sound recording equipment and covert listening devices. Sound amplifiers and amplified microphones allow private investigators to hear sound from a distance.

    http://www.spygear4u.com/listening-devices.asp?PARTNER=applied5564

- **Nanny Cams** - Hidden cameras used for keeping tabs on babysitters and nannies while you're away. Includes wireless nanny spy cams, hidden nanny cameras, mini cams and more.

    http://www.kqzyfj.com/click-5444568-10922785

- **Night Vision Binoculars** - Night vision goggles, binoculars, and weapons sights. Useful for night time surveillance and security.

    http://www.einvestigator.com/spy_equipment/night_vision_binoculars.htm

- **Private Investigator Equipment** - Advanced spy equipment for private investigator's and detectives including digital camcorders, voice recorders and cameras, portable receiving and recording surveillance systems, auto voice recorder and note pad, digital binoculars, jacket camera, covert video systems, bug detection kits, undercover jackets, and watch voice recorders.

    http://www.spygear4u.com/pi-gear.asp?PARTNER=applied5564

- **Police Officer Equipment / Police Gear** - Spy and surveillance equipment gear for police officers, cops, law enforcement. Includes such security products as: Handcuffs, breathalyzers, hidden cameras, metal detectors, bug detectors, GPS tracking devices, police gear, and more

    http://www.spygear4u.com/police-gear.asp?PARTNER=applied5564

- **Security Gear** - Personal security and home security devices and equipment

    http://www.spygear4u.com/security-products.asp?http://www.spygear4u.com/police-gear.asp?PARTNER=applied5564

- **Self Defense** - Self defense products and weapons for your own personal and home security such as: tasers, stun guns, personal alarms, mace, pepper spray, batons, and more.

    http://www.spygear4u.com/self-defense-products.asp?PARTNER=applied5564

- **Spy on Cell Phones** - Learn how to spy on wireless phones and mobile phones, get data from cell phones, text messages, instant messages and more.

    http://www.einvestigator.com/spy_equipment/spy_on_cell_phones.htm

- **Spy Equipment Accessories** - Miscellaneous accessories, electronic equipment

    http://www.spygear4u.com/accessories-spy-gear.asp?PARTNER=applied5564

- **Survival Kits and Survival Accessories** - Survival kits and various survival accessories
  http://tinyurl.com/survivalnations

- **Video Systems** - Electronic video equipment including: packaged camera systems, CCTV and DVR monitors
  http://www.spygear4u.com/cctv-video-recorders.asp?PARTNER=applied5564

- **Video Recorders** - Video surveillance equipment for recording subject activity, video spy equipment and other cheap spy gear
  http://www.spygear4u.com/cctv-video-recorders.asp?http://www.spygear4u.com/cctv-video-recorders.asp?PARTNER=applied5564

http://www.anrdoezrs.net/click-5444568-10749928

Computer vs. Internet Forensics

The widespread use of computer forensics resulted from the convergence of two factors: the increasing dependence of law enforcement on computing (as in the area of fingerprints) and the ubiquity of computers that followed from the microcomputer revolution. As computer forensics evolved, it was modeled after the basic investigative methodologies of law enforcement and the security industry that championed its use. Not surprisingly, computer forensics is about the "preservation, identification, extraction, documentation and interpretation of computer data." In order to accomplish these goals, there are well-defined procedures, also derived from law enforcement, for acquiring and analyzing the evidence without damaging it and authenticating the evidence and providing a chain-of-custody that will hold up in court. The tools for the "search-and-seizure" side of computer forensics are a potpourri of sophisticated tools that are primarily focused on the physical side of computing: i.e., tracing and locating computer hardware, recovering hidden data from storage media, identifying and recovering hidden data, decrypting files, decompressing data, cracking passwords, "crowbarring" an operating system (bypassing normal security controls and permissions), and so forth. For those who are old enough to remember the original Norton Utilities for DOS think of these modern tools as the original Norton Disk Editor for DOS on steroids.

The Battle is Fierce

"Tell me; where is cyberspace? Point out to me exactly where it is.

Show me the billion of airwaves coursing through our bodies and surroundings non-stop 24/7.

You have a website? Reach out and touch it for me.

Reach out and pluck a fax from the air. Or reach out and pluck the photo of your kid that you just sent grandma out of the air and show it to me.

Where is the Internet? And where are the billions of bits of information sent at seemingly light speed around the world. Show them to me.

The text message you sent…where did it go and how did it get there?

Show me the software you just downloaded and installed on your computer. Not the interface that pops up on your computer screen but show me the bits and bytes that make it work.

It is all AIR!!! It is nothing more than air. Every day we all buy, send and use air and every day we all do not realize that our lives are changing as new technology is released and as becomes a major part of our lives."

So begins my book on mobile commerce called, "Selling Air":

http://www.amazon.com/dp/B006JOIS5K

Scientists tell us that air is good for us and it is! We cannot live without air. But "air" can also be harmful to us and this "harmful air" is what this course is all about.

The Internet is a fantastic medium and worldwide community connection but inherent evil lurks in the background where you cannot see it. Evil people look for every opportunity to wreak havoc on your business as well as your person. Everything from spying on your cell phone to network intrusion and hacking…the bad guys are out there and patiently waiting to ensnare another victim…and some of them are smart…very smart!

The Internet provides a global network of communication and also a venue for deceptive marketing and advertising. From advertisers selling you cheap Viagra, to scammers promising you Nigerian Money Offers, to being announced the monthly winner of a foreign Lottery Club; you may wonder if anybody is out there going after the perpetrators of these scams. The short answer: YES, there is! But there aren't enough of us and that is where you come in.

Here is just a partial list of things to watch for:

- **Online Auctions:** Misrepresented or undelivered goods
- **General Merchandise:** Misrepresented or undelivered goods not purchased through auctions

- **Fake Check Scams:** Consumers used fake checks to pay for sold items, and asked to have the money wired back
- **Nigerian Money Offers:** Deceptive promises of large sums of money, if consumers agreed to pay the transfer fee
- **Lotteries:** Asking winners to pay before claiming their non-existent prize
- **Advance Fee Loans:** Request a fee from consumers in exchange of promised personal loans
- **Phishing:** Emails pretending to represent a credible source, ask consumers for their personal information (e.g. credit card number)
- **Prizes/Sweepstakes:** Request a payment from consumers in order for them to claim their non-existent prize
- **Internet Access Services:** Misrepresentation of the cost of Internet access and other services, which are often not provided
- **Investments:** False promises of gains on investment

"You don't know how good the good news is until you first know how bad the bad news was!"

I will first show you how bad the Internet is and then demonstrate to you just how easy it is to protect yourself and your family from the cyber den of thieves. Are you ready? Then let's get at it now...

And you think you have problems?

How it all started - Internet History

Let's begin at the beginning. Many of my readers have no idea how and when the Internet came into being. I began on the Internet when it became available to the general public in 1989 and immediately saw the immense opportunity it offered. But at the same time, dirt bags from all over the world saw the same opportunity to deceive naïve people and as I learned all about the Internet and computers...they did too! So, from the beginning, the battle lines were drawn. And the war is brisk! The following was taken from Wikipedia...

Email

E-mail predates the inception of the Internet, and was in fact a crucial tool in creating the Internet. MIT first demonstrated the Compatible Time-Sharing System (CTSS) in 1961.

It allowed multiple users to log into the IBM 7094 from remote dial-up terminals, and to store files online on disk. This new ability encouraged users to share information in new ways.

E-mail started in 1965 as a way for multiple users of a time-sharing mainframe computer to communicate. The ARPANET computer_network made a large contribution to the development of e-mail.

There is one report that indicates experimental inter-system e-mail transfers began shortly after its creation in 1969. Ray_Tomlinson initiated the use of the "@ sign" to separate the names of the user and their machine in 1971. The ARPANET significantly increased the popularity of e-mail, and it became the killer app of the ARPANET.

Internet

The **Internet** is a global system of interconnected computer_networks that interchange data by packet switching using the standardized Internet Protocol Suite (TCP/IP). It is a "network of networks" that consists of millions of private and public, academic, business, and government networks of local to global scope.

The Internet carries various information resources and services, such as electronic mail, online chat, file_transfer and file sharing, online_gaming, and the inter-linked hypertext documents and other resources of the World_Wide Web (WWW).

A 1946 comic science-fiction story, A Logic Named Joe, by Murray Leinster laid out the Internet and many of its strengths and weaknesses. However, it took more than a decade before reality began to catch up with this vision.

The USSR's launch of Sputnik spurred the United States to create the Advanced Research Projects Agency, known as ARPA, in February 1958 to regain a technological lead.

The first two nodes of what would become the ARPANET were interconnected between UCLA and SRI_International in Menlo Park, California, on October 29, 1969.

Use of the term "Internet" to describe a single global TCP/IP network originated in December 1974. During the next nine years, work proceeded to refine the protocols and to implement them on a wide range of operating systems.

The first TCP/IP-based wide-area network was operational by January 1, 1983 when all hosts on the ARPANET were switched over from the older NCP protocols. In 1985, the United States' National Science Foundation (NSF) commissioned the construction of the NSFNET.

The opening of the network to commercial interests began in 1988. The US Federal Networking Council approved the interconnection of the NSFNET to the commercial MCI Mail system in that year and the link was made in the summer of 1989.

Other commercial electronic e-mail services were soon connected. In that same year, the first three commercial Internet service providers (ISP) were created; important, separate networks that offered gateways into, and then later merged with, the Internet.

Various other commercial and educational networks were interconnected with the growing Internet. Telenet (later called Sprintnet) was a large privately funded national computer network with free dial-up access in cities throughout the U.S. that had been in operation since the 1970s. This network was eventually interconnected with the others in the 1980s as the TCP/IP protocol became increasingly popular.

The ability of TCP/IP to work over virtually any pre-existing communication networks allowed for a great ease of growth, although the rapid growth of the Internet was due primarily to the availability of commercial routers, the availability of commercial Ethernet equipment for local-area networking and the widespread implementation of TCP/IP on the UNIX operating system.

Growth

Although the basic applications and guidelines that make the Internet possible had existed for almost a decade, the network did not gain a truly public face until the August 6, 1991. The World Wide Web was invented by English scientist Tim Berners-Lee in 1989.

On 25 December 1990 he implemented the first successful communication between an HTTP client and server via the Internet. Berners-Lee is the director of the World Wide Web Consortium (W3C), which oversees the Web's continued development.

An early popular web browser was ViolaWWW, patterned after HyperCard and built using the X_Window System. It was eventually replaced in popularity by the Mosaic web browser. In 1993, the National Center for Supercomputing Applications at the University of Illinois released version 1.0 of Mosaic, and by late 1994 there was growing public interest in the previously academic, technical Internet.

By 1996 usage of the word *Internet* had become commonplace, and consequently, so had World Wide Web. Meanwhile, over the course of the decade, the Internet successfully accommodated the majority of previously existing public computer networks.

Some likely scenarios

I am going to describe for you some likely scenarios that are taken from our case files. These are just a few things Internet Forensic Investigators face daily.

Title: The Suicide Stalker

Case File Number 200808-001-FN-6

Synopsis: In August 2008 a woman, under the moniker of Johnny B Goode, began accessing teen chat rooms and posing as a young male teenager. Over an 8-month period, she was responsible for 4-teen suicide deaths caused by cyber-bullying. Law Enforcement was unable to determine her identity or her location. She operated through a series of offshore proxies based in China and then only through computers she hijacked effectively hiding her identity and location. ForensicsNation was hired by one of the parents of the victims to hunt this stalker down and bring him/her to justice. This is how we hunted her down and put an end to her reign of terror.

August 8, 2008 – hired to hunt down the Suicide Stalker

August 11, 2008 – contacted the 4-chat rooms where Jonny B Goode was registered and where all 4-victims had met her. All 4-chat rooms agreed to cooperate in catching the Suicide Stalker.

August 12, 2008 – Installed ForensicsNation software probe code named "Newman". Newman is a virtual watch dog that plants himself inside any computer system or network (we will not tell you how or where) and sits and watches silently. When a hacker or intrusion of any kind is detected by Newman, he plants himself inside the perpetrator's computer and watches to see what other cyber-crimes the perpetrator is committing as it begins to gather evidence. Newman can break through any proxy and any defense that a perpetrator attempts to hide behind and deliver the evidence to ForensicsNation to eventually be turned over to law enforcement. Newman is the best and he hasn't ever been defeated. You can run but you cannot hide because Newman will find you no matter what it takes.

August 13, 2008 – Newman reports a target and in the process of sending data the perpetrator shuts down her computer. This is highly perplexing; Newman has never been discovered since Newman disguises himself as a .dll file extension and is not visible to even the best anti-virus and spyware programs but the facts speak for themselves. The ForensicsNation team assembles to discuss what could have happened. In the course of the discussion two facts emerge: 1) the perpetrator is a highly skilled computer person. 2) The perpetrator must have been watching her outbound bandwidth transmission and discovered something was communicating outbound so she shut the computer down.

August 14, 2008 – taking into consideration that the perpetrator knows that she has been penetrated, we continue to watch the 4-known chat rooms while ForensicsNation investigators make contact with 12-other well know teen chat rooms and explain the investigation to them. All of them with the exception of one chat room agree to allow ForensicsNation to scan their operations on a 24/7 basis. Newman is installed on all 11-chat rooms and programmed NOT to communicate back to ForensicsNation except at start-up when the perpetrator turns her computer on and then only in a burst transmission which takes about a nanosecond. If the perpetrator is watching, she will not be able to see any outbound activity.

August 16, 2008 – After scanning all chat rooms for over 48-hours, ForensicsNation determines that the perpetrator is not a registered member under another name. At this point, all efforts are directed to new member registrations. ForensicsNation personnel begin scanning all new member registrations dating back to August 13, 2008.

August 18, 2008 – ForensicsNation personnel discover a new registration under the moniker "FreakyB" is using the same offshore proxy setup as Johnny B Goode. Newman is programmed to penetrate FreakyB when she next signs on.

August 22, 2008 – ForensicsNation personnel begin to become concerned that somehow FreakyB has discovered she is being monitored but since Newman has not made a penetration because she has not signed on, ForensicsNation personnel sit patiently and wait.

August 24, 2008 – Newman reports a target when FreakyB signs on to one of the chat rooms and immediately goes to sleep and lays dormant. ForensicsNation personnel monitor FreakyB's activities as she engages numerous teens in a chat. After 16-minutes, FreakyB signs off.

August 28, 2008 – Newman transmits in a burst transmission the IP-address and location of the perpetrator's computer and then immediately shuts down. Perpetrator's computer is located in Falls Church, VA. Newman determines that perpetrator is using an air card issued by Verizon under the name of Stanley Kidderman but at a different address in Suffolk, VA. Law Enforcement officials are notified and both jurisdictions send out detectives to both addresses. Two facts emerge from the detective's reports: 1) Stanley Kidderman is a retired fireman with lung disease and was not aware that his air card was lost or stolen. His live-in nurse stated that he is an active computer user and the detectives asked if he would voluntarily submit to having his computer searched. Kidderman grants his permission. Subsequent investigation of the Kidderman computer by law enforcement analysts revealed that Kidderman is not the perpetrator. 2) The Church Falls address belonged to a Mrs. Carl Knudsen, a widower and pensioner that rarely uses her computer but leaves it on 24/7. Mrs. Knudsen also consented to a voluntary computer search and it was determined that the Knudsen computer had been hijacked. To ForensicsNation personnel, the perpetrator is hijacking computers to remain hidden. It is also obvious to ForensicsNation personnel that the perpetrator is one smart cookie and takes no chances. With the consent by both Kidderman and Knudsen, Newman is installed on both computers.

September 3, 2008 – Newman transmits a new target with an IP-address and location in Norfolk, VA. Follow-up investigation by ForensicsNation personnel reveals the same scenario – a hijacked computer.

September 11, 2008 – all activity by FreakyB in the aforementioned chat rooms has ceased. Newman has not reported any new target for over a week. The ForensicsNation team assembles to discuss this new development. It is obvious that subsequent to both investigations of the Kidderman and Knudsen computers, the perpetrator has become aware of law enforcement zeroing in on his/her activities. This could explain the sudden cessation of FreakyB activities. The mystery remains on how perpetrator found out about law enforcement's actions.

September 12, 2008 – ForensicsNation's sister company – Applied Mind Science – sends a behavioral scientist to profile the perpetrator. After reviewing all chat room logs and communications, the AMS doctor determines that the perpetrator is a woman disguised as a young teenage boy.

September 13, 2008 – the ForensicsNation team assembles and determines that Kidderman's live-in nurse is now a viable suspect. She was present at the time detectives made their inquiry of Kidderman. A call is made to Kidderman requesting the nurse's cell phone number. At this time Kidderman reveals that he owns the cell phone and pays the monthly bill but has never used the phone. He gives permission for ForensicsNation personnel, to place a laser GPS tag on the phone and ForensicsNation personnel begin scanning past text messages and call patterns.

September 15, 2008 – ForensicsNation's investigation of the nurse's cell phone revealed the following: 1) She conducted very few text messaging and only to her children. 2) The majority of her cell phone voice calls were to businesses providing services to Kidderman with very few personal calls. 3) There were two calls made to toll free numbers for periods over 20-minutes. 4) Investigation of these toll-free numbers using a toll-free number owner identifier reveals that both numbers were to computer dial-up companies. Because of what the investigation revealed, Kidderman's nurse is now the prime suspect.

September 17, 2008 – FreakyB reappears in one of the chat rooms. ForensicsNation personnel immediately conduct a scan Kidderman nurse's cell phone to see if it is in use. It is not but the scan also reveals that the phone is turned off and the battery removed since the GPS function is not working completely. Note: a cell phone's GPS can be turned off from the cell phone's menu but not completely. The GPS function will still remain available for emergency services. The only way to completely turn off a cell phone's GPS is to remove the battery. Newman once again transmits new target info and again after subsequent investigation, it is another hijacked computer.

September 18, 2008 – ForensicsNation personnel question Kidderman again about the whereabouts of his nurse at the time of FreakyB coming online. Kidderman informed ForensicsNation personnel that his nurse had the day off and was not present in his home. Kidderman was not aware of her whereabouts on any of her days off but confirmed that she leaves for the day and doesn't return until the following morning.

September 19, 2008 - ForensicsNation team assembles to discuss the latest developments. There is now no doubt in any of the team member's mind that Kidderman's nurse is FreakyB. Team members make contact with Kidderman and again request permission to place a GPS tracking tag on the nurse's cell phone. Kidderman grants permission and a laser tag is placed on the phone. Note: a laser tag is placed by calling the target phone number and marrying the tag to the phone even if the phone is not answered.

September 20, 2008 – Kidderman confirms that his nurse's next day off is September 23rd.

September 23, 2008 – Kidderman's nurse departs for her day off. She is tracked to the public library four blocks away from Kidderman's home. Immediately FreakyB signs on to one of chat rooms. Law enforcement is called in and sent immediately to nurse's location. Nurse is detained and the library's computer is confiscated as evidence.

September 24, 2008 - ForensicsNation team receives a call from law enforcement personnel that an analysis of the library's computer reveals that the nurse was not online with a chat room as FreakyB but was online on Skype chatting with her daughter. Nurse is released without being charged. ForensicsNation team assembles to discuss this amazing development. If Kidderman's nurse is not FreakyB then who is? And how can it be explained that FreakyB logged on to the chat room at the exact same time the nurse was chatting with her daughter? Suspicion is now cast on the daughter and the team orders an investigation of the daughter.

September 25, 2008 – ForensicsNation personnel make contact with Kidderman and request any information about the nurse's daughter. Kidderman is of no help and does not know the daughter nor has he ever met her. A search of the daughter's Skype registration information reveals only that she lives in Atlanta, GA and her first name of Francine. A check of Skype's computer logs reveals an Atlanta, GA IP-Address and the cable carrier that provided ISP services to the daughter. A further check of the ISP's data files reveals the daughter's first and last name, her home address and her occupation – COMPUTER PROGRAMMER FOR IBM.

September 27, 2008 – ForensicsNation team members make contact with IBM security personnel and request permission to place Newman on her office computer. IBM security personnel are highly doubtful that daughter would use her work station to commit cyber-stalking but grants permission. Note: Throughout the investigation all times and log-ons for FreakyB show that a good majority of them were during business hours where suspect would be at work. This fact alone was enough to sway IBM security personnel to allow Newman.

September 29, 2008 – Librarian at the library that nurse was using to talk to daughter on Skype calls ForensicsNation team and informs them that the nurse has just logged on to another library computer. ForensicsNation team checks and immediately sees that FreakyB logs in to one of the chat rooms. Newman reports a target identifying the daughter's work station communication with library computer using Skype and also logged into chat room. We got her. The Suicide Stalker is the daughter. ForensicsNation team notifies IBM security and law enforcement and daughter is arrested and her computer confiscated.

September 30, 2008 – While under interrogation daughter reveals that her mother participated in the stalking. Nurse/mother is arrested.

Case Closed October 2, 2008

Statistics on Internet Fraud

The Internet Crime Complaint Center (IC3), a joint venture of the FBI and the National White Collar Crime Center found:

- Online auction fraud was the most reported type of fraud and accounted for 44.9% of consumers' complaints
- Non-delivered merchandise and/or payment made up 19.0% of complaints
- Check fraud represented 4.9% of complaints
- About 70% of the fraud victims were scammed through www (e.g. online auctions)
- About 30% of the victims were scammed by emails

<u>**Payment Methods**</u>

Top methods of payment used by victims of Internet fraud include:

- Wire
- Credit Card
- Bank Debit
- Money Order
- Check

The average loss for all Internet frauds was $1,500. More than half of these losses occurred through auctions. So protect yourself from becoming the next victim of an auction fraud. Read the tips on how to prevent auction frauds from happening to you.

Tips on How to Prevent Auction Frauds

- Learn as much as you can from the seller
- Read and examine the feedback on the seller
- Check the location of the seller. If the seller is abroad and a problem arises it will be harder to solve.
- Ask if shipping and delivery are included in the price so you receive no unexpected or additional costs.
- Refuse to give the seller your social security number or driver's license number to prevent identity theft. In fact get used to saying "no" to information requests on the Internet.

Some noteworthy observations:

(1) HelpAssistant, and "Support" accounts and passwords ship with XP - there's no way to get rid of these accounts - hmmmm.

(2) LC4 does the "cracking" on the old LAN Manager (LM) hash technology inherited from OS/2 which is relatively trivial to break. NTLM passwords involve a relatively robust password hashing algorithm, but that advantage is removed by default because XP automatically converts NTLM to the easily breakable LM hash for backward compatibility. Given enough time, LC4 will break every LM hash, so the "fix" is to disable the LM hash capability in the Registry and sacrifice the backward compatibility.

(3) We ran LC4 on this workstation for a bit over 16 days (67% of a complete run), and recovered all but 3 passwords. (4) Three of the passwords were cracked in less than 1 second!

(5) LC4 can be deployed over a network!!

Listed below are some common categories and a few examples of computer forensics toolkits:

1. File Viewers: Quick View Plus (http://www.jasc.com)
2. Image Viewers: ThumbsPlus http://www.cerious.com)
3. Password Crackers: l0phtcrack or LC4 (http://www.atstake.com)
4. Format-independent Text Search: dtsearch (http://www.dtsearch.com)
5. Drive Imaging: Norton Utilities' Ghost (http://www.symantec.com)
6. Complete Computer Forensics Toolkits:
    1. Forensics Toolkit (http://www.foundstone.com);
    2. ForensiX (http://www.all.net);
    3. EnCase Forensic (http://www.encase.com)
7. Forensic Computer Systems: Forensic-Computers (http://www.forensic-computers.com)
8. One of the more full-featured network tools, NetScanTools Pro (http://www.netscantools.com). Note the abundance of features built into one product!

Most computer forensics vendors offer a variety of tools, some even offer complete suites. But the links above will provide a useful, high-level overview of the world of computer forensics and the tools used therein. A cursory review of this list suggests tools that are not mainstream for the typical computer villain.

Now the rubber meets the road. We observed that the impetus for computer forensics came from law enforcement - a community that arrests, investigates, seizes, stores and locks up physical objects. The computer forensics specialist's adversary, in all likelihood, is a computer-using criminal with no particular skill level beyond that of a typical end-user. Such is not the case with Internet Forensics

A cursory review of this list of computer forensics tools suggests that they are not in widespread use by the typical computer villain. The pornographer might use a graphics tool to morph the images into something unrecognizable immediately, but that's unlikely to be anywhere near as challenging as doing a reverse-morph on an unknown file format. The computer forensics specialist works on a different plane than the person he/she is investigating.

To the contrary, the Internet Forensics specialist uses many of the same tools and engages in the same set of practices as the person he/she is investigating. Let me illustrate with a few examples.

Suppose that you've received some suspicious email, and want to verify the authenticity of a URL included within. A number of options are available. One might use a browser to access information from the American Registry for Internet Numbers (http://www.arin.net). Or one might use any number of OS utilities. But we'll save ourselves some time and worry, and use a general network appliance, NetScanTools Pro. We identified the registration, domain name servers, currency information, etc. for netscantools.com.

Now let's change the scenario slightly. Suppose that we had some hostile intent, and wanted to ferret out information about some company's network infrastructure. What tool might we use? You guessed it, NetScanTools Pro. The point is that the self-same tool is equally useful to the hacker conducting basic network reconnaissance and the legitimate Internet security specialist who's trying to determine whether a URL links to a legitimate company or a packet "booby trap." The point is that, both uses require essentially the same skill sets.

Don't get me wrong, I am not suggesting that NetScanTools Pro is a hacker tool. It is a general-purpose network analyzer. I use it all the time to analyze my networks and to explain network analysis issues to my students. But in order to serve in that capacity, it must also have the capabilities to be misused by hackers. In Internet Forensics it is customarily the case that the forensic specialist undergoes the same level of education and training as the hacker he or she seeks to thwart. The difference is one of ethics, not skill. We observed that this was not true of the perpetrator and investigator in computer forensics.

To drive home the point, look at the other options that NetScanTools Pro provides. One can use an ICMP "ping" to identify whether a particular network host is online just as easily as one can use it to identify activity periods in network reconnaissance or a network topology. One can use a Traceroute to determine network bottlenecks, or to identify intervening routers and gateways for possible man-in-the-middle attacks. One can use Port Probe to verify that a firewall is appropriately configured, or to make a list of vulnerable services on a host that may be exploited.

Where computer forensics deals with physical things, Internet forensics deals with the ephemeral. The computer forensics specialist at least has something to seize and investigate. The Internet forensics specialist only has something to investigate if the packet filters, firewalls and intrusion detection systems were set up to anticipate the breach of security. But, if one could always anticipate the breach, one could always block it. Therein lies the art, and the mystery.

If I've been successful, I've got you thinking about the fundamental differences between computer forensics and internet forensics. I think that on careful analysis, one has to conclude (a) that these are fundamentally different skills, (b) that in the case of Internet forensics, the skill sets of the successful perpetrator and successful investigator are pretty much the same, and (c) Internet forensics is as much a discipline as its search-and-seizure counterpart. This validity of these conclusions may be confirmed in any number of ways. For the most part the tools-of-the-trade for both hacker and Internet forensics specialist are the same, though the occasional extreme case like Dug Song's Dsniff http://monkey.org/~dugsong/dsniff challenges this generalization. It's hard for me to imagine a legitimate, lawful use of Dsniff's "macof" utility that enables the users to flood switch state tables! But in the main, the hacker and the Internet Forensics specialist could co-exist with the same tools and equipment.

There is also a parallel in the flow of the network traffic. Ingress traffic to the analyst is egress traffic to the hacker, v.v. The same packet crafting technique that verifies true stateful inspection of fragmented packets also launches exploits like Teardrop and Ping of Death. Indispensable tools for packet capture and analysis like tcpdump are, by definition, capable of promiscuous packet sniffing, as are intrusion detection systems like Snort. The underground hacker community and the Internet folks with the white hats are birds-of-a-feature if one ignores the direction of their moral compass. This is the time to change our focus from the negative (hacker) to the positive (Internet Forensics Specialist) dimension of this exciting new discipline, and to begin to take the differences between computer forensics and internet forensics seriously. To make the distinction complete, we need to add a few publications in Internet Forensics as SANS has already achieved near perfection in the conference arena, and GIAC already has established certification standards that seem to be universally accepted.

If we can break from the tradition of including Internet Forensics (under some name or other) as the penultimate chapter of a Computer Forensics textbook, and mislabeling the excellent word already done in the field under the theme of "reverse-hacking" we'll be well on our way to completely articulate Denning's durability, body of principles, body of practices and standards for competence, ethics and practice tests for a genuine profession.

Useful tools for the "Amateur Investigating Sleuth"

I going to give you some "amateur" tools to help you become an "amateur" Internet investigator" that will assist you in finding the bad guys when they attempt or succeed in finding you.

Forensic Tools:
File Viewers: http://www.jasc.com

Image Viewers: http://www.cerious.com

Password Crackers: http://www.atstake.com

Format-independent Text Search: dtsearch: http://www.dtsearch.com

Drive Imaging: Norton Utilities' Ghost: http://www.symantec.com

Forensics Toolkit: http://www.foundstone.com

ForensiX: http://www.all.net

EnCase Forensic: http://www.encase.com

Forensic Computer Systems: http://www.forensic-computers.com

NetScanTools Pro: http://www.netscantools.com

Who owns a phone number?

The fastest, easiest and simplest way to find out who owns any phone number is Phone Search Central: http://www.phonesearchcentral.com/

If you want to do things the harder way (which is NOT worth the time), FoneFinder; http://www.fonefinder.net will tell you which company owns the phone number. You can then subpoena that company to get the owner of the phone number.

Address and phone of a person

PeopleFinders: http://www.peoplefinders.com is a reasonable service. Their "people search subscription" works reasonably well, finding all sorts of things, including some things that are completely wrong. Don't use this for 800 number reverse searches...I never got anything even remotely useful from those (and they will reverse the charge on these automatically if you make a mistake). For cell phone numbers doing a reverse search, it will tell you only the name of the subscriber; and the location of the number when it was originally assigned; no address of the person. It is annoying that on every search it prompts you to sign up for a $16.95 "savings" program. The link to sign up is huge. The link to say "no thanks" is below it in small type, and somewhat hard to find. I did a criminal search on a guy I knew was convicted and it wouldn't tell me what county it was in, but it did find it. This service is a bit pricey, but may be your lowest cost option if you've exhausted the alternatives.

How to find out the merchant ID of the company

You may have to put a small $ transaction through in order to get complete info. Having a rejected transaction may only give you the "name" of the vendor as it would appear on your statement which can be quite obscure and often bogus.

Bank of America ShopSafe: https://www.bankofamerica.com/banking-information/faq/credit-cards/faq.go is the best option. You can generate a onetime number (including the 3 digit code) that is tied to your credit card and you can set a dollar and time limit on that unique card number. But once a merchant charges to that card, it is locked to that merchant. So it is really safe.

A Visa Buxx: http://usa.visa.com/personal/cards/prepaid/visa_buxx.html number or a **Visa reloadable card like this one below:**

http://usa.visa.com/personal/cards/prepaid/prepaidcard.jsp?it=l2|/personal/cards/prepaid/visa_buxx.html|Visa%20Reloadable

Keep the amount in the account really low. When they try to charge your card, you can find out their merchant ID but ONLY if the transaction goes through! If it doesn't go through, then you only get the info that would appear on your bill (which could be bogus and it is not traceable). There are monthly fees though even if you don't use these cards. The B of A ShopSafe has no additional fees.

Tracking down violators
http://www.tcpalaw.com/free/track.htm

This page at tcpalaw.com is an excellent resource of all sorts of information including forms to get PO Box information.

Recording phone conversations

I use Personal call Recorder from www.digital-loggers.com. I use the free WavePad from www.nch.com.au and sample at 16000 and save it in MP3 Constant bit rate CBR 16kbps (high quality). For lower quality and fast saves, capture at 8K and save in .wav format, PCM, 8kHz, 8 bit, mon, 7Kb/sec. Be sure it is legal first; each state has different laws regarding taping a phone conversation without the other caller being aware that he/she is being taped.

900 numbers
Number Administration System

http://www.nanpa.com/nas/public/form900MasterReport.do?method=display900MasterReport shows the responsible organization for each number. You then send a subpoena to the company to find out who owns it.

800 number ownership

As far as finding the resp org (responsible organization), in theory your long distance carrier should be willing to supply that for you. Ameritech has an automated service at 800-337-4194; they typically give a service number associated with the RespOrg, which you can then call to find out who the RespOrg actually is. A third method: "If you don't know who to subpoena, use the RespOrg services or go to:

http://www.fonefinder.net (Note: this works for non-toll free numbers too!) and find out the provider and then go to:

http://www.nanpa.com/number_resource_info/carrier_id_codes.html

(Download the "Feature Group D CIC assignments" zipfile) to get their contact info. Call to ask who to send a subpoena to, and then send it.

If you have a login, you can go right to the source: http://www.sms800.com

For Canadian numbers: see CO Code Availability:

http://www.cnc.ca/mapcodes.htm

With respect to subpoenas to RespOrg, I've found that you can generally fax the subpoena to them and simply ask that they fax the answer back. In three of three cases, they have simply faxed the information back to me.

Phone number ownership
Abika services: Find out who owns a number or who is calling you:

http://www.abika.com/Reports/FindPhoneNumbers.htm

Abika offers a very comprehensive set of searches and is very similar to Docusearch. Unlike Docusearch they can trace the source of a fax call into your phone number. This is the only service we know of that lets you do that without your having to change your incoming fax line into an 800 number (they can't block their callerID if you have an incoming 800 number).

The way their service works is that you forward your fax line to their number and they forward the call back to your number instantly. In the process, they pick off the callerID that you can't get. So let's say you get 10 faxes a day. You just note the time you receive each fax and correlate it to the list they give you of phone numbers that called you at the same time. So you can identify the number of every single fax you got over any time period! It's called the "Trace Phone Calls" Search.

The Abika "Trace Phone Calls" service is highly recommended because you get the phone numbers of each of the junk faxers that called you regardless of how they are trying to block their number. Then you can use the other Abika searches to find out who they really are (billing name and address, etc). Then you can sue the sender of the faxes. This is particularly useful for pump and dump faxes and the 900 number "we want your opinion" faxes because these faxes generally never identify who is sending them (since they want to avoid lawsuits) and if they have an opt-out number, it is generally http://www.blocklist.com and that's totally useless since blocklist doesn't identify individual clients...they just give the list to all their clients. So you can't sue blocklist and blocklist can't tell you who sent the fax. In fact, someone can just list the blocklist numbers and not even be a blocklist client! So that's why the Abika service is so important and it's the only one we know of that does this.

The cost is $79.96 ($69.98 plus 9.98 processing charge) for the first month; $10 for 1 month extensions. You get 100 minutes of talk time free with your initial order. You can buy additional 60 minutes of talk time for $10 each. For Canada, Hawaii, Alaska and Puerto Rico you get 50 minutes of talk time free with your order. You can buy additional 30 minutes of talk time for $10 each.

Note: You will probably not be able to forward back to the original number. This will depend on the local phone or Cell Phone Company and often on the area, even within the same phone company. They have a database of the phone/cell companies and the areas where it works and it does not. For areas where it gives a busy signal the call has to be returned to a different phone number or voicemail.

But for fax lines, if you don't have a second line handy or a fax machine that timestamps when the fax was really received (I don't have either), the best option is to do what I did and just forward my fax number to Abika's call center and then have them forward it the phone number of an efax service you sign up for such as http://www.efax.com. So you don't have to have another phone line installed, and you get an electronic record of everything, including accurate receipt times that you can then correlate to their call logs. And you can set everything up instantly (the efax number is instant; call forwarding may take a couple of business days to add).

Abika can immediately tell you of the caller's origin number and billing address. You either call or email them for the info. This is part of the "Trace Phone Call" monthly service. So to do a live trace, you must do the same as described above, i.e., forward your number to them and have it forwarded back. As long as the call is 5 seconds or longer, you'll know who called you.

The service works virtually 100% of the time, even if the number is "out of area" or blocked and even when they were unidentifiable by callerID, *69, and *57. Basically, they get the ANI (Automatic Number Identification) information that certain businesses get. Getting ANI delivered real-time to your home or office requires installation of digital equipment and a separate digital line, and programming at the CO. So Abika is the quick and easy way to accomplish the same result (getting the ANI information), but without the hassle, cost, or time delay.

Here's what they write:

> We have had hundreds of customers who have used our call trace. If you would like to test us out, I can activate trace for a number you specify and you can ask any of your associates to dial that number from any unlisted, anonymous phone number or even using *69 and check us out. We will trace the origin number for all calls that originate in US and Canada. The proof is in the pudding. The test will speak for itself. (Can we get the $20 for winning the bet?)
>
> Regarding our price list, we do not have fixed pricing of our products. Our prices are dynamic and vary according to the complexity of the various searches we offer. Where is the price list? Each search is unique and gets the attention it requires. Prices vary depending on whose and what information you are searching as some information is easier (cheaper) to search and some more difficult (expensive). Once you fill out the search form with the search criteria and click "next" you will see the prices for that particular search. If the information is easy to search then that particular search is listed as FREE! You can try any of our searches. **All of them have a money back guarantee for inaccurate information found.** As a businessperson you would be interested in knowing that the Wall Street Journal got the full report on Richard Scrushy (ex CEO) of Healthsouth's suspect activities from us even before anyone else in the media or investment community suspected anything. The time when WSJ got the full report Healthsouth was a high flying stock. In most of the searches we offer, we have the best sources for the information. We have even had a senior editor of People Magazine, a few magazine reporters and news anchors of a couple of local TV stations use us to get information for some of their stories and personal needs.

Here are some testimonials from customers who agreed to publish their feedback: http://www.abika.com/help/feedback.htm

> You may be interested to know that we offer a similar service to trace emails and instant messages. Emails and IM traces are available for the whole of N. America, W. Europe, India, South Africa and the Pacific Rim Countries including Australia and Japan.
>
> I wonder when many of the so called tech gurus say that emails and IM's are untraceable. We have conducted thousands of these traces with a success rate of more than 98%. A few major corporations use us to trace emails and IM's.

If you have any more questions or need any more information please do not hesitate to contact us online. help@abika.com. Or if you choose you can call us at: 720-207-0362.

Docusearch: http://www.docusearch.com/

Use Docusearch to lookup License plate owners, social security numbers lookup (for creditors) and find out who owns an 800 number, regular phone number, and more. Expensive (well under $100), but some stuff you can only get this way. If they can't find it, there's no charge. Also use Ameritech's automated RespOrg ID service: 800-337-4194.

Call trap procedure

This is guaranteed to get your offender. Have the phone company put a "trap" on the line, make note of when the calls came in. You must have the EXACT time of each call. Then I report it by calling the Annoyance and Tracking line. For SBC, the number is 800-698-7223. After you get two faxes from the same sender, if they can't get a number, then they can put traps at the remote location and eventually you get them. Hit 0 to speak a live person when calling the SBC number.

Here is some more info on call trap: Caller ID and My Privacy:

https://www.privacyrights.org/fs/fs19-cid.htm

The number for the SBC Annoyance call bureau is 925-867-8101, for example. Here's some slightly conflicting advice: Now *all* calls are logged by the LEC's (Local Exchange Carrier) computers. Ask them (via subpoena) for a call detail report (CDR) for all calls into and out from your number on the affected date. *ALL* the phone companies have this data... most for 90 days of history or more. If they tell you they don't, they are lying

Accurint.com: http://www.accurint.com/

25-cents a search. Highly useful for tracking down people, even with unlisted phone numbers. Accurint uses a name, past address, phone number or Social Security Number to obtain the current name, address and phone number of targeted subjects. Be careful that you don't lookup someone you don't have a legal reason to lookup, or you can be sued by that person. So if you are looking up information for a lawsuit, that's ok.

Whois Source - Wildcard Domain Search Lookup
http://www.whois.sc/

I have a silver membership here. It's totally worth it if you look up website registration. There are other lots of other reverse lookup tools here if you are a member.

Advanced Research, Inc. - Background Investigations, Asset Searches, Telephone Records, Locates: http://www.advsearch.com/

They will find a bank account owned by the debtor, bank balances for all accounts in a given bank, bank transactions, credit card transactions, Canadian phone records, etc. Even international bank account searches. You can find out where the person is currently employed. Searches that is not available on the traditional databases.

MelissaData address lookups:

http://www.melissadata.com/Lookups/index.htm

Lookup address related thing

Ancillary Service Endorsements:

http://w5.melissadata.com/cgi-bin/search.asp?pnf=appnotes/ancserv.htm

"Return service requested" (preferred) or "Address service requested" is both ways to find a new address or confirm an existing address. See this page for a description of each type of endorsement.

Free People Search - Find People - Free People Locator - Find People Free, Skip Tracing, Trace People at skipease.com variety of people search: http://www.skipease.com/

Find anyone! We'll locate missing persons, debtors, assets, and employment (skiptracepros.com): http://www.skiptracepros.com/ Pay service but worth it.

Satellite photos - You can search by latitude/longitude, street address, zip code, or well known locations:

http://mapper.acme.com/

http://terraserver.microsoft.com/

International business name search

General Guides: Company Registrars - Register of Companies - Trade, Industry

http://www.scottishlaw.org.uk/corporate/registrars.html

International Company name search

http://www.damonlegal.com/link_to_forms.htm

International phone number search

International phonebooks directory

http://www.phonebooks.com/international-phone-book.html

International Telephone Numbers Directory - City, State, Country Phone Number Look-up

http://www.searchdetective.net/International_phone_number.html

Batch reverse phone number

Use Accurint batch mode or a service from infoUSA.com.

http://list.infousa.com/cgi-bin/abicgi/abicgi.pl?bas_session={bas_session}&bas_elements=4&bas_vendor=190000&bas_type=LC&bas_page=6999&bas_action=dataproc

ABA number lookup

ABA routing number verification. Free bank routing number search tool:

http://yourfavorite.com/checkwriter/verify.htm

Bank account balance: See if funds are in the account you want to levy!

http://bettercheck.com/

TCPALaw investigation tools

A great list: Tracking down violators

http://www.tcpalaw.com/free/track.htm

Report bogus domain information

Bogus information in the domain registration in violation of ICANN regulations. Registrars are required to ensure that registration data is complete & accurate. You will have to subpoena the registrar for the information on who paid for the registration. You should also download and capture all information off of the web site and look to see who hosts the web page, as they can also be subpoenaed for customer data. In the meantime, you can report incomplete or inaccurate domain registration information here: http://wdprs.internic.net/

CorpAmerica Corporate filings

http://www.corpamerica.com/cam/Error.html?pageNotFound=%2Fcam%2Fproducts%26_services%2F

If you want to find out who the officers are, etc. you can order a "plain" copy of corporate records for any state in the US and some foreign corporations. See also: Division of Corporations - Authorized Direct Web Vendors:

http://www.corp.delaware.gov/directwebvend.shtml

Yellow pages, white pages, and reverse number lookup:

http://www.anywho.com/

http://www.argali.com/

Forward and reverse phone number lookup. This is a downloadable FREE tool that searches public databases.

FCC unsolicited fax orders and search:

http://transition.fcc.gov/eb/tcd/ufax.html

Enter the name your favorite spammer and read what the FCC has done about them. Our favorite spammer, fax.com has 6 separate FCC citations on this page alone! This site uses the search engine that I invented when I was CEO of Infoseek, by the way. The FCC citations explain the law much better than anything I've seen on other sites. Read a few of them to educate yourself on the law.

GEEKTOOLS Whois Proxy

http://www.geektools.com/whois.php

Fast whois lookup

Cell Phone Magic:

http://www.cell-phone-numbers.com/

They will find out who owns a cell phone.

This online store offers a variety of searches and stuff you won't find anywhere else....like how to get keys for the car you want to levy. http://www.ioffer.com/

US SEARCH: http://www.ussearch.com/consumer/index.jsp

Similar to Docusearch

Offering nationwide and international investigative services, spy gadgets, safety and surveillance products, records research, criminal background checks and personal information verification services. Information retrieval for insurance companies, law firms, repossession agents, financial institutions, collection agencies, private investigators, bounty hunters, process servers, bail bondsmen, businesses, spouses and parents.

UPS Store Locator/ mail drop mailbox mail box location

Actually what you ALWAYS do when you have any address of any perpetrator is simply first go to the UPS Store Locations search page

http://go.vicinity.com/upsnew/prxStart.dsp

http://go.vicinity.com/mbe/prxStart.dsp

http://www.semaphorecorp.com/cgi/form.html

Excellent maildrop search: Mail boxes - remailing services. Directory of mail drops and mail boxes: http://www.maildropguide.com/go/

Who is at this Address?

If I have an address and I am not sure what it is, or if it's even a real address, then I always go to http://www.usps.com and look up the address and the post office that delivers to the address. Then I call that post office and ask them if they know what's located at that address. I ask if it is a residential address, or if it's an office building of some sort. I ask them if they know if the address is a Commercial Mail Receiving Agency (CMRA) like a Mailboxes Etc or UPS Store. The post office is not required to answer these types of questions, but they can if they want to. I'd say 90% of the time they tell me what I need to know.

FEIN number lookup

Federal Employer ID Number can found here if it is registered:
http://wwwKnowx.com

FEIN Number information Search Corporation Tax ID Number

https://www.knowx.com/fein/search.jsp Otherwise http://www.dnb.com may work.

AutoTrackXP: https://clear.thomsonreuters.com/

Very comprehensive searches! Requires a subscription agreement and qualification.

Reverse Phone Directory - Find Name and Street Address from Telephone Number

http://www.reversephonedirectory.com/

Reverse phone number lookup:

http://www.infospace.com/ispace/ws/index

Find out who owns a phone number

Reverse Address Directory - Lookup Street Address Find Person's Name and Telephone Number to Locate People and See Who Lives There.

http://www.reverseaddress.com/

Craig Ball's Sampler of Informal Discovery Links:

http://www.craigball.com/hotlinks.html

A pretty extensive list of resources

ScreenNow: https://screennow.lexisnexis.com/pub/

Get all sorts of info on a person.

Net Detective 2001 people search utility software- HDP Corporate Website

http://ndet.jeanharris.com/

Essentially a bunch of semi-useful hyperlinks, all categorized for you

OnlineDetective.com - unlisted phone numbers dmv records detectives personal public records investigate anything and more!

http://www.onlinedetective.com/

Seems to be similar to net detective

SuperPages.com: http://www.superpages.com/

A search at superpages.com (hint: I usually look for the category "mail" at the particular address, then if that doesn't turn up a mail drop, search for any businesses at the address) turns up, for example, 5401 Chimney Rock Apartments 5401 Chimney Rock Road, Houston, TX 77081 (713) 661-3790

Canada phone number lookup

http://www.canada411.ca/

Canada's 411

United States Postal Service - ZIP + 4 Lookup

https://www.usps.com/

Handy when they don't give you enough info to confirm you got the right company.

GNU wget: http://www.gnu.org/software/wget/wget.html

I used this to grab a complete copy of the fax.com website so that they couldn't change it.

Find out who owns a PO Box: http://www.junkfax.org/fax/misc/pobox.htm

Some popular techniques to find out the owner of PO Box

Telephone Prefix location: http://www.thedirectory.org/pref/

If you have a phone number like (650) 423-xxxx, it will tell you where that phone is.

CCS International Ltd: Surveillance, Counter surveillance and Hi-Tech Spy and Security Products: http://www.spyzone.com/

GSM, CELLULAR, COMPUTER, FAX MONITORING

http://www.gcomtech.com/

Due to federal law, you must be in law enforcement to get access to this site.

ZoomInfo: http://www.zoominfo.com/

This is a free site where you can find lots of information about a person or a company gathered from analyzing web pages. Very impressive!

Find out who called you

Use the call trace feature offered by the phone company. I did a *57 and got a "successful" trace, FWIW, plus an announcement that for $8 (plus tax and tip, no doubt) I can even have it reported to the police. For $8, they can record the number. Then if you take action, you subpoena the phone company for the call info, and if it is a subscriber of that phone company, you get info on the caller as well. If it's not a subscriber of the phone co, you generally get who the local carrier is so you know who to subpoena for the subscriber info. If you were to have the number but want the subscriber info, and issued a subpoena to SWB, they would charge you a $25 fee for the record search. When you do a call trace, you get the whole shebang for $8. I've done call traces when I have the subscriber's name and number, but want a) a sworn affidavit from the phone company saying that the call was made from number "X" to my number "Y" at a specific date and time, and b) if it is from a SWB customer, full ID of the calling party, including name & address where the service is installed. All for $8, much cheaper than issuing a subpoena for records after the fact, and with more info.

Locating a company

http://www.residentagentinfo.com page links to all the state corp. search pages on the net. Pretty helpful, if you still can't find it

http://www.checkemout.com/corporation_go.html has a nationwide corp/dba search for $39.00.

http://www.freelancesecurity.com will let you have private PI's bid for a service you describe.

Can We Tape: http://www.rcfp.org/taping/

Rules regarding taping of phone conversations in each state.

Subpoena information

The AT&T Subpoena Center 800-291-4952 (voice) 248-552-1764 (fax)

Southwestern Bell, SBC is now AT&T Teleport Communications Group (TCG) is now AT&T Corporate Security (Subpoena Compliance) 800-732-5689 800-559-7928 (general information) Must mail subpoena to: AT&T c/o CT Corporation Systems 1515 Market Street, Suite 1210 Philadelphia, PA 19102

I was told that they charge $150 for subscriber information, but that they will refund that money if they simply rebill service to another telephone service provider. One time they looked up a number that I gave them on the phone and told me it was rebilled to ICG Telecom Group, so I didn't need to send a subpoena at all.

Southwestern Bell, SBC is now AT&T Pac/Pacific Bell is http:www.sbc.com, 800-750-2355 Subpoena Department is 800-291-4952 (1, 5) 208 S. Akard, 10th Floor Dallas, TX 75202 214-464-2854 (fax) They said that they won't respond to a civil subpoena from out of state unless I have a search warrant or make a request on a federal level.

AT&T long distance and RespOrg information 877-973-7767, 2 Send subpoena's for toll free numbers to VP Regulatory Long Distance 5850 West Los Positas Boulevard, Room 302 Pleasanton, CA 94588 I sent a subpoena to AT&T the West Los Positas address and it was responded to by SBC Southwest at the South Akard address. I also sent one that never got a response.

Online Resources

Center for Democracy and Technology. *Impact* of the *McCain-Kerrey* Bill on *Constitutional Privacy Rights*.

http://www.cdt.org/crypto/legis_105/mccain_kerrey/const_impact.html

CERIAS: Digital Forensics Resources.

http://www.cerias.purdue.edu/research/forensics/resources.php?output=printable

Computer Crime and Intellectual Property Section Criminal Division, United States Department of Justice. Sear*ching* and Seizing *Computers* and Obtaining *Electronic Evidence* in Criminal *Investigations*.

http://www.cybercrime.gov/s&smanual2002.htm

Computer Forensics, Cybercrime and Steganography Resources

http://www.forensics.nl/links/

Computer Forensics World.

http://www.computerforensicsworld.com

Computer Professionals for Social Diversity: Computer Crime Directory.

http://www.cpsr.org/cpsr/computer_crime

Cornell University. *Federal* Rules of *Evidence*.

http://www.law.cornell.edu/rules/fre/overview.html

Craiger, J. Philip. Computer For*ensics Procedures* and Methods.

http://www.ncfs.ucf.edu/craiger.forensics.methods.procedures.final.pdf

Forensics Information from CERT

http://www.cert.org/forensics/

The Forensics Science Portal

http://www.forensics.ca/index.php

Ghosh, Ajoy. *Guidelines* for the *Management* of *IT Evidence.*

http://unpan1.un.org/intradoc/groups/public/documents/APCITY/UNPAN016411.pdf

Kessler International - Forensic Accounting, Computer Forensics, Corporate Investigation.
http://www.investigation.com/praccap/hightech/compforen.htm

National Center for Forensic Science.

http://www.ncfs.ucf.edu/digital_evd.html

Nolan, Richard, et. al. *Forensics* Guide to Incident Response *for Technical Staff.*

http://www.cert.org/archive/pdf/FRGCF_v1.3.pdf

Robbins, Judd. An Explanation of C*omputer Forensics.*

http://www.computerforensics.net/forensics.htm

Sergienko, Greg S. *Self* Incrimination and *Cryptographic Keys.*

http://law.richmond.edu/jolt/v2i1/sergienko.html#h1

Printed Resources

Casey, Eoghan. *Digital* Evidence *and* Computer Crime (Second *Edition).* San Diego, CA: Academic Press, 2000.

Farmer, Dan; Venema, Wietse. *Forensic Discovery.* Addison-Wesley Professional, 2005.

Nelson, Bill. *Guide* to Computer *Forensics* and *Investigations.* Boston, MA: Thomson Course Technology, 2004.

Forensic Resources

Site Name or Subject	Description
FINDING PEOPLE *FOR FREE*:	
Directory Services:	
Craig's Phone Finder http://www.craigball.com/phonefind.html	Performs parallel search of other directory services, including Yahoo, WhoWhere, Switchboard, Infospace, AnyWho and Worldpages, plus reverse searches by phone # or address and map links.
MelissaData Lookup Directory http://www.melissadata.com/Lookups/index.htm	This eclectic melange of lookups isn't going to make you Sherlock (or Shirley) Holmes,

	but it's a useful compendium of free data. Thanks to Lee Keller King for the suggestion
AnyWho http://www.anywho.com/	A simple, fast way to search over 100 million directory listings. More up-to-date than some. Reverse directory too.
Bankruptcy Locator http://www.merlindata.com/search/bankonfr.html	This free search will tell you whether the individual or business name you enter is listed in a bankruptcy filing since January 1992. This search will tell you the date, name, city and state.
Bigfoot	So-so white pages, yellow

http://www.bigfoot.com/	pages, web pages and e-mail searches.
Information USA http://www.abii.com/	Listings for 113 million households and 10 million businesses
Info Space http://www.infospace.com/	Search telephone directories in USA, Canada and other countries. Also yellow pages search, E-mail finder, corporate directory, Toll free number database, fax number database, and government telephone number directory. An excellent, wide-ranging site.
LYCOS People Finder	Search a massive

http://www.lycos.com/peoplefind/	telephone database
Switchboard http://www.switchboard.com/	A simple, quick way to find almost anyone, anywhere who has a listed phone number.
WhoWhere http://www.whowhere.com/	Find E-mail addresses and phone numbers from among 90 million U.S. listings. Also, toll-free numbers, yellow pages and corporate web site locator
WorldPages http://www.worldpages.com/	Links to 112 million U.S. and Canadian white and yellow pages listings, but most valuable for its links to over 200 directories worldwide.

YAHOO People Search http://www.yahoo.com/search/people/email.html	Conduct surname searches via a national cris-cross directory. Locate E-mail addresses, home pages and phone numbers.
Reverse Directory Services:	
Reverse Directory: InfoUSA http://bit.ly/nsPDa1v	Both a people finder and a reverse directory: If you know the phone number, this database will return the subscriber's name and address
Reverse Directory: InfoSpace http://bit.ly/rkKrVW	This directory offers reverse lookup by phone number, fax number, U.S. street address and e-mail address!

Reverse Directory: DM411 http://bit.ly/mVsL4M	Another reverse directory that will return the subscriber's name and address when you input the phone number
Resources for Finding People:	
Birthday Database http://anybirthday.com/search.htm	Over 130 million birthdays online in a free searchable database. Search by name, limit by zip code.
Social Security Death Index http://bit.ly/mWTHez	Find information about persons whose death triggered a Social Security benefit (e.g., social security number, dates of birth and death and place of residence).

Black Book Online http://www.crimetime.com/online.htm	A helpful, free collection of links to investigative resources warns that it is "for professional investigators ONLY. If you are not a private investigator, or in the legal, insurance, collection, journalistic or law enforcement professions."
Search Systems Public Record Locator http://www.searchsystems.net/	This comprehensive links list is free, well-organized and includes many gems. It's definitely worth a look.
"Searching for People" page http://www.searchingforpeople.com/	Links to resources for finding people
Missing Persons Resource	Articles and

Center http://www.pimall.com/nais/missingm.html	book descriptions on professional methods for skip tracing.
Webgator http://www.virtualgumshoe.com/	Excellent list of online investigative resources
FEE BASED INVESTIGATIVE RESOURCES	
Accurint http://www.accurint.com/	The newest kid on the block for skip tracing. What sets it apart is not just the high quality of its data, but its pricing: just dirt cheap. Accurint can find people for a quarter and will deliver a neat little dossier of addresses, relatives, neighbors and more in seconds, for under five

bucks. The interface is intuitive and intelligent, and the system allows users to track usage by account or client number and authorize use by others within an account. The owner of the account can set additional user IDs and passwords, as well as program access limits for authorized sub-users. Although currently geared to not much more than skip tracing, UCC filings and phone numbers, Accurint expects to be adding drivers' license records for thirty-three states along with

	criminal records data. On a scale from one to wow, Accurint is a WOW!
Public Data http://bit.ly/qP387e	This inexpensive but increasingly dated database contains records of licensed drivers, sex offenders, voters, vehicle license tags, criminal records and voter rolls. Search license records by name or DL # and learn name, address, weight, birth date, sex, expiration date, status, class and restrictions. Although principally a Texas resource, it also offers DMV and/or DL information for Florida, Idaho,

	Iowa, Maine, Mississippi, Minnesota, Ohio, Oregon, South Dakota, Utah and Wyoming.
Flat Rate Info http://www.flatrateinfo.com/	If you are a bulk user of skip trace and dog tag data, this powerful site may be a good bet. True to its name, FlatRateInfo.com allows subscribers unlimited access to its database of credit headers, property ownership, phone numbers, etc. for a single flat rate. But, with annual subscription rates starting at $1,400.00, the service only

	makes sense for those conducting thousands of searches per year, in such fields as collections, mailing list updates and HR departments at large organizations. If you have the budget and the volume, this is a great tool.
URAPI http://www.urapi.com/	Texas only. The new kid on the block offers a few bells and whistles not found on PublicData.com, including a handy "tag records" feature. Although they claim that URAPI (you-rap-ee) stands for "Uniform Rapid

	Assessment of Public Information," what an amazing coincidence that it also sounds like "You are a P.I." Pricing is painless ($20.00 for 200 searches), but they still need to work out some of the bugs.
US Search http://www.ussearch.com/	This heavily-publicized company does a reasonably good job of skip-tracing and background checking. They are pleasant and helpful, while offering a very quick turnaround and live telephone support outside regular business

	hours.
Information for Business http://www.info4business.com/	A reliable resource with reasonable prices and toll-free telephone support. This well-run outfit offers just about any type of data you could want and an impressive turnaround time for basic reports. The helpful people give this service an edge. Highly recommended.
American Information Network http://www.ameri.com/	Purchase reports re: bankruptcies, birth records, business background info, credit reports, death records, driving records, education verification,

	employment history, financial information, judgments, skip trace, media reports, pleasure craft/FAA registrations, criminal records, professional licensure, property ownership, tax liens, etc.
Dataland http://www.dataland.com/	This attractive and well-organized site offers the full range of skip-trace and asset identification data. Be warned that some of the data they are offering for sale is currently available online without charge (e.g., Social Security death records, surname

	searches, OSHA reports, FAA records, etc.).
Texas Department of Public Safety Convictions Records Database http://records.txdps.state.tx.us/	This site allows you to obtain information about criminal conviction and felony deferred adjudication records maintained by the Texas Department of Public Safety. Courts and criminal justice agencies throughout the state submit these records to DPS. Searches cost $3.15 each and you can pay online with a credit card.
InformUs http://www.informus.com/	Driving records nationwide, Workers' comp. claim searches in 40 States,

	criminal records nationwide, previous employment verifications in 72 hours, national credit and address information.
	FREE to check validity and state/time of issuance for any S.S. #.
KnowX http://www.knowx.com/	A reasonably priced (and partially free) search engine for millions of public records, including real property ownership, bankruptcies, assets, UCC filings and many more.
Locate Fast http://www.loc8fast.com/	Claims to have a *billion* records online. $1.75 per

	credit header search (name, SS#, address, phone).
LocateMe http://locateme.com/	Search selected public records (principally voter and DMV records) of all 50 states for $39.00 per search.
National Association of Investigative Specialists http://www.pimall.com/nais/home.html	A fascinating conglomeration of investigative resources, spy equipment, skip trace resources, P.I. publications, etc.
SEARCH ENGINES	
Craig Ball's Search Central http://www.craigball.com/searchcentral.html	Use all major search engines via one simple interface. Not selling anything!
Google http://www.google.com/	This is the best search engine in the world. A very

	fast, often relevant search engine that is less likely than some to be misled by metatags and other techniques used to draw users to sites.
Dogpile http://www.dogpile.com/	This inelegantly-named site permits simultaneous searches of every part of the Internet using all major search engines
All The Web http://www.alltheweb.com/	More than 200 million URLs indexed and very fast search capabilities.
Alta Vista http://www.altavista.digital.com/	Key word searches
Yahoo	Topical search engine. Very

http://www.yahoo.com/	user friendly.
Beaucoup http://www.beaucoup.com/	Extraordinarily comprehensive links to all manner of search engines (over 800 listed) and reference sources. Perhaps the ultimate in one-stop searching.
Savvy Search http://www.savvysearch.com/	Another parallel search engine that allows you to check 17 major search resources in one fell swoop.
SEARCH NEWSGROUPS AND MAILING LISTS	
Google Groups (formerly deja.com) http://groups.google.com/	Search through Email in USENET newsgroups and mailing lists for specific subjects. You can sift through more than

	40,000 discussion forums, plus newsgroups and mailing lists (700,000,000 messages!).
CHECK OUT CORPORATIONS AND ASSOCIATIONS	
Tax Exempt Organizations http://1.usa.gov/ne64fS	Search the IRS' directory of tax exempt organizations by name, city and state.
Hoover's Corporate Information http://www.hoovers.com/	Profiles of corporations (some free, some fee-based) and relevant links. An excellent first stop for corporate information.
Lexis http://www.lexis.com/	The old familiar legal research tool is a superb way to identify

	the registered agent for service of process and other key information about any registered corporation, PA or PC. Goto TXSOS (for Texas Secretary of State Records) (Fee based). You can search Lexis and Nexis via the Internet if you are a current subscriber by using the URL: **telnet://nex.lexis-nexis.com/** Tell them your terminal type is ".vt100"
SEC EDGAR Archives http://www.sec.gov/cgi-bin/srch-edgar	Online corporate filings with the U.S. Securities and Exchange Commission.

61

Tx. Sect'y of State Records http://ecpa.cpa.state.tx.us/coa/coaStart.html	The Texas Comptroller of Public Accounts offers access to selected (and in my experience incomplete) Texas Secretary of State corporate information, between the hours of 7 a.m. and 10 p.m. CT, Monday through Friday. Lexis does a much better job, but this information is free.
Report Gallery http://www.reportgallery.com/	Many links to corporate annual reports and web sites
CHECK OUT INSURANCE COMPANIES	
A. M. Best http://www.ambest.com/	Address, phone number and rating for insurance

	companies
Insurance Company Locator http://www.compuwork.com/company.html	Names, addresses and phone numbers for about a trillion insurance carriers
Insure.com http://www.insure.com/index2.html	Ostensibly unbiased consumer information about auto, home and life insurance, including insurance company ratings from Standard & Poor's. Includes insurance links by state and a library of carrier lawsuits.
Texas Dept. of Insurance http://www.tdi.state.tx.us/index.html	Many useful items here, including lists of authorized insurers and agents, disciplinary

	actions and consumer rights information.
CHECK OUT LAWYERS	
State Bar of Texas Attorney Database http://bit.ly/pakfYb	Obtain the registered data, current license status and State Bar Number or all Texas attorneys.
The Bluesheet http://bit.ly/pakfYb	Online guide to verdicts and settlements in Texas, New Mexico, Kansas, Missouri and Louisiana (free and fee based resources available)
Martindale-Hubble http://www.martindale.com/	The online version of the ubiquitous lawyer's decorative books. MH lets you find just about any

	lawyer in America.
Texas Electronic Ethics Reporter http://www.lawlib.uh.edu/ethics/	Online ethics opinions
West's Legal Directory http://bit.ly/nqSy8p	Offers basic information on over 800,000 lawyers. Yikes!
PLANES, TRAINS, BOATS, TRUCKS & AUTOMOBILES	
Aviation Databases http://bit.ly/n2j5Ae	An extensive collection of searchable databases of aircraft ownership, registration, pilot licensure, etc.
Coast Guard Vessel Database http://bit.ly/pOW5ix	Search the United States Coast Guard's database of vessels (crafts >5tons) by vessel name. To search by vessel I.D. number,

	click [here]().
[Commercial Interstate Carriers](http://www.safersys.org/)	Search the Department of Transportation's SAFER database. Searchable by firm name, DOT Number and Motor Carrier number. If you catch the D.O.T. number stenciled on the cab of a tractor trailer, you can use this database to get the truck's owner, insurance carrier, and crashes in the last two years.
[Air Transport data](http://www.bts.gov/oai/)	The Bureau of Transportation Statistics Office of Airline Information (OAI) database

Airworthiness Directives http://av-info.faa.gov/ad/AD.htm	Contains malfunction and defect reports on aircraft and parts.
NTSB Accident Briefs http://www.ntsb.gov/NTSB/query.asp	A searchable database of National Transportation Safety Board aircraft accident briefs
NHTSA http://www.nhtsa.dot.gov/cars/	National Highway Traffic Safety Administration. Regulations, standards, recalls and a host of other automotive safety information.
NHTSA Recalls http://1.usa.gov/pm1AVR	Information on recalled vehicles, organized by year and model.

US Dept. of Transportation http://www.dot.gov/	Handsome site links to government agencies with oversight function for trains, planes, automobiles and boats. Search a massive library and regulatory database. A great resource.
Accident Reconstruction Resources http://www.c-design.com/accrec.html	Extensive list of Internet links, addresses and phone numbers of accident reconstruction resources, including reconstruction software packages
Kelly Blue Book http://www.kbb.com/	How much is that car worth? FREE online access to the massive market value database (both wholesale

	and retail values available)
PRODUCTS LIABILITY, ET AL.	
Chemical Health & Safety Data http://1.usa.gov/qazj5Y	Toxicity and Safety data on chemicals of every stripe. Sponsored by the National Institute of Environmental Health Services
ATSDR http://bit.ly/p34GTI	The Agency for Toxic Substances and Disease Registry offers Data on toxic and hazardous substances
Standards and Specs http://bit.ly/oyVEaB	Comprehensive links to standards for just about anything you can imagine.
U.S. Dept. of Labor's Occupational Safety & Health	Complete OSHA standards

Admin. http://www.osha.gov/	online, plus links to other safety and health sites.
Material Safety Data Sheets http://msds.pdc.cornell.edu/msdssrch.asp	Alphabetical compilation of Material Safety Data Sheets for virtually any compound.
Consumer Product Safety Commission http://www.cpsc.gov/	The US Consumer Product Safety Comm. shares recall info and publications. This site is especially good for toy safety advisories.
Construction Criteria Base http://www.ccb.org/	An online construction industry library detailing codes, standards, specification and documentation of every stripe pertaining to the construction industry.

	Subscription only except for free access to the Unified Facilities Guide Specifications.
The Consumer Law Page Defective Product Resource Page http://bit.ly/mUVaLp	This useful compilation of resources (primarily geared to promote California's The Alexander Law Firm), offers a host of information about defective products and lists many links to other resources.
Intellectual Property Resources http://www.patents.com/resource.htm	"One stop shopping" for online patent and trademark resources
Delphion Patent Server http://bit.ly/qSiuED	Database of millions of U.S. Patent & Trademark

	Office patent descriptions from 1971 to present, and graphics from 1790 to present. Search for patents by number or by words in the inventor, title, abstract, assignee, agent, and claims fields. Each patent links to all others in that classification. Also contains data on foreign patents. Limited free access.
MEDICAL	
Craig's Managed Care Links http://www.craigball.com/hmo/index.html	A concise list of links of use to persons litigating managed care liability cases.
American Medical Association	Offers online member

http://www.ama-assn.org/	database
PubMed http://www.ncbi.nlm.nih.gov/PubMed/	The Nat'l Library of Medicine gives FREE access to the 12 million+ citations in MedLine.
Medscape http://www.medscape.com/	Medscape offers free access to Medline, Toxline and Merriam-Webster's Medical Desk Dictionary, as well as tens of thousands of full-text articles covering a range of medical specialties. An excellent, fast-growing and easy-to-use resource. Think of it as "Yahoo M.D."
Merck Manual http://www.merck.com/pubs/mmanual/	The Merck Manual of Diagnosis and Therapy, now in

	its 17th edition, is the best all-around medical reference source out there. Thank you Merck & Co.
New England Journal of Medicine http://www.nejm.org/	Non-subscribers have access to abstracts of online articles back to 1975 and full text of articles more than six months old.
The Visible Human http://www.nlm.nih.gov/research/visible/	They froze some folks solid, scanned the heck out of them, sliced them up thinner than pastrami and photographed it all. An amazing, massive database of anatomical information and stunning

	pictures.
BANKING	
American Bankers Association http://www.aba.com/	One of American banking's most influential lobbying organization. Banking links, products, services and professional education.
List of Bank Internet Sites http://128.242.221.170/Banks/index.html	This site claims to link to over 95% of all online bank sites.
American Banker Online http://www.americanbanker.com/	Headlines, financial data and a free two week trial subscription.
Federal Reserve Bank of Dallas http://www.dallasfed.org/	The official home page of the Dallas Fed, "the Banker's Bank." Offers publications, economic data

	and links to other Fed resources.
Federal Deposit Insurance Corporation http://www.fdic.gov/	This comprehensive site offers much of use to commercial bankers, including downloadable FFIEC forms, full-text searching of FDIC rules and regulations and detailed financial data on individual banks (making it easier to keep an eye on the competition).
National Information Center http://www.ffiec.gov/nic/	The Fed's National Information Center of Banking Information. Offers data on bank

	organizational structures and finances.
Currency Exchange Rates http://www.uta.fi/~ktmatu/rates.html	Daily unofficial average cross rates for major international currencies. Slick, but easy to use.
Banking Law Online http://www.law.cornell.edu/topics/banking.html	Why waste money on high-priced lawyers? Free online access to the text of Federal and state bank regulations and federal appellate decisions. Read it and you'll quickly realize why you hire the lawyers.
Bank Rate Monitor http://www.bankrate.com/	Geared to consumers of banking services, offers mortgage, home equity loan,

	savings, credit card and checking account rates. Also tracks ATM fees and online banking fees for >2,500 institutions, surveyed weekly in 117 mkts and 50 states.
Credit Unions http://www.ncua.gov/	The National Credit Union Administration is an independent federal agency that supervises and insures 6,814 federal credit unions and insures 4,181 state-chartered credit unions.
ACCOUNTING	
Texas Society of Certified Public Accountants http://www.tscpa.org/	The TSCPA hosts an excellent webpage

	offering information on CPE programs, an archive of "Today's CPA" magazine articles, member news and a concise but well-selected links page.
SmartPros Accounting http://www.accountingnet.com/	Billing itself as "the complete online resource for accounting professionals," this energetic site includes an online research facility and a thriving forum for accounting professionals (recent topic: "Are accountants stuffy or is it me?"),
American Institute of CPAs http://www.aicpa.org/	Conference information, a wealth of online

	publication and industry news and a comprehensive links page save this otherwise dry-as-dust site.
AuditNet Resource List http://www.auditnet.org/	An excellent overview of online accounting resources. If it's in English, on the 'Net somewhere and concerns accounting, it's probably listed here.
IRS Tax Forms and Publications http://bit.ly/ptGDUH	If forced to say something nice about the Service, I'd mention its website. All the major reporting forms and publications are online here, in Adobe Acrobat (PDF) "file

	ready" format.
IRS Tax Regulations http://1.usa.gov/o9NJiLI	Although not the easiest site to navigate, the regulations are all here.
Texas Tax Codes http://www.capitol.state.tx.us/statutes/txtoc.html	Plain and simple site links to the full text of the various Texas tax codes.
Texas Taxes http://www.window.state.tx.us/m23taxes.html	With links to reporting forms in Adobe Acrobat (PDF) format and much useful tax data, this is one of the best state-sponsored sites around.
MAPS	
Expedia Maps http://www.expediamaps.com/	Microsoft modestly calls this site "the best resource for online maps." It's not. I guess if

	the map is wrong, Bill Gates buys the town and moves it.
MapQuest http://www.mapquest.com/	Free atlas, personalized maps of any location and driving directions
Map-Related Websites http://bit.ly/pWw23P	Comprehensive list of online map resources. This is a map lover's paradise!
MapBlast http://www.mapblast.com/	Another good site that gives you a map if you give it an address, or even an intersection.
TerraServer http://www.terraserver.microsoft.com/	Online free satellite imagery of virtually every place in the U.S. and many populated locations throughout the

	world.
TRAVEL	
Savvy Traveler http://www.dianaball.net/	Okay, I'm biased. This is my wife's link site, but that doesn't change the fact that it's an intelligent and handy resource for the savvy traveler (or the person who wants to be one).
Concierge.com http://www.concierge.com/	The online realm of Conde Nast Traveler magazine. A lovely photo gallery, useful online forums and editor's choices make this site special.
Expedia http://www.expedia.com/	Microsoft's online travel planner. It offers some fine

83

	features, including flight status information and 360 degree travel views.
Fodor's Travel Online http://www.fodors.com/	An excellent site, especially useful for locating restaurants and hotels and for travel tips. But, you have to wonder why Houston --the 4th largest city in the US-- is omitted entirely!
Frommer's http://www.frommers.com/	This "Outspoken Encyclopedia of Travel" principally promotes the many books and resources in the Arthur Frommer series. Still, very useful.
Rick Steves' Europe Through the	Public TV's

Back Door http://www.ricksteves.com/	goofy travel guru knows his stuff when it comes to enjoying Europe on the cheap. Pack light and check this site (especially the comments in the "graffiti" section) before you go.
Realtime Flight Tracking http://www.flytecomm.com/cgi-bin/trackflight	Free, up-to-the-minute data on planes in flight between major U.S. cities. Superimposed on a weather map. Very cool!
Travelocity http://www.travelocity.com/	Good all-round general database and a good place to start to check flight connections, prices and availability.
Yahoo Travel	Yahoo's portal to travel

http://travel.yahoo.com/	information is characteristically simple and includes reservation links. Although it boasts a few travel goodies, this site remains little more than a search engine, and only tangentially a content provider.
HOUSTON LINKS (you can find any city listings like the ones below by using Google.com)	
Houston CitySearch http://houston.sidewalk.citysearch.com/	Slick and savvy guide to movies, restaurants, art & music and entertainment in and around the Houston area
Harris County Appraisal District http://www.hcad.org/	HCAD offers on-line appraisal information and maps, searchable by name, address or account

	number. Business, personal and mineral property too.
Houston Area Weather http://bit.ly/ngfuak	Local weather observations and forecast. Includes current radar and satellite views.
Houston Area Realtime Traffic http://traffic.tamu.edu/traffic.html	This page is a bona fide glimpse into the future. Cars with transponders are electronically interrogated at 1 to 5 mile intervals along freeways and HOV lanes. Their speed data is sent to a central computer that calculates travel times and builds this Internet map.

Houston Chronicle Online http://www.houstonchronicle.com/	Houston's "leading Information source" has staked out its corner of the Web. A searchable archive of more than ten years of the late Houston Post and the Chronicle is available online.
Houston Code of Ordinances http://bit.ly/nXju7S	The City of Houston's Code of Ordinances is online at this site.
HPD Crime Statistics http://bit.ly/nsv6GC	Interested in a detailed breakdown of all the reported major crimes in your Houston neighborhood? Check out the Houston Police Department's Crime Stats page. It's a bit

	cumbersome to figure out your police beat, but the data should be less than three weeks old.
Lake Conroe Webcam http://www.ballpoint.org/webcam.html	A real-time view out the window of the Ball family lake house on Lake Conroe: "Houston's Playground." Just for fun.
DALLAS LINKS (you can find any city listings like the ones below by using Google.com)	
North Dallas Chamber of Commerce http://www.ndcc.org/	The North Dallas Chamber serves as a forum for discussion and action on the vital issues of the business community and helps promote the development and continued success of its members.

Dallas Area Rapid Transit (DART) http://www.dart.org/default.asp	DART on the Web. Slick site offers system maps and service info.
D/FW Air Traffic Control http://www.caesimuflite.com/atcindex1.html	Listen to LIVE conversations between air traffic controllers and pilots of aircraft arriving and departing the Dallas-Fort Worth area.
Yahoo's Guide to Dallas/Fort Worth http://dfw.yahoo.com/	Comprehensive guide to D/FW Internet resources. The best place to start.
Dallas Morning News http://www.dallasnews.com/	Read the top stories in the morning paper and search past issues.
Dallas Weather http://www.wfaa.com/weather/index.html	Live link to WFAA Dallas storm track

	radar
Dallas Fire and Police Scanner http://www.policescanner.com/	Listen to LIVE Dallas police and fire department scanner broadcasts. Car 54 where are you?
Southwest Airlines http://www.iflyswa.com/	Is there another way to get in and out of Dallas? If you buy your tickets online, you receive double flight credit on the RapidRewards program. Thanks Herb!
MISCELLANY	
Texas Appraisal Districts Online http://www.craigball.com/appraisal.html	A hyperlinked list of more than sixty Texas county appraisal districts that have their records online. A

	simple, quick way to find people and assets.
Texas County Data http://www.txcountydata.com/	Billed as "Texas' Largest Online Property Record Database," this excellent site offers free, detailed searches (by owner name or property address) of real property ownership and appraisal data for 27 Texas counties. The database includes Montgomery and Fort Bend counties, but Bexar, Dallas, Harris, Tarrant and Travis counties are notably absent. For Harris County property

	records, use http://www.hcad.org
State Records http://www.crimetime.com/bbostate.htm	A hyperlinked directory of a variety of state records online--mostly corporations, licenses and real estate.
FEDEX http://www.fedex.com/us/tracking/	Track FedEx packages by airbill number. Query: If you get something from the opposition, can you run *sequential* airbill numbers to see *to whom else* they are sending FedEx packages? Probably a real bad idea, ethically speaking.
UPS	Track any UPS bar-coded

http://www.ups.com/	shipment and find out where it is at this very moment.
E-Bay http://www.ebay.com/	What can I say? I'm an e-Bay junkie. This online auction lists over 3.8 million items for sale. A cautious buyer can get incredible deals. If you collect anything, e-Bay will likely prove the best, cheapest source for what you seek.
Political Contributions http://www.tray.com/FECInfo/index.html-ssi	Search Federal Election Commission records of political contributions. Which way do you suppose the judge leans if she gave $1,000.00 to

	"The Newt?"
Automatic Translator http://world.altavista.com/tr	You've got to love this! Enter any text, or even the URL of a web page, and this free service automatically translates it to or from Spanish, French, German, Italian or Portuguese.
Webcams http://www.steveweb.com/80clicks/	One of many Webcam link pages. "Around the World in Eighty Clicks" links to real-time images of people and places all over the world.
FACSNET http://www.facsnet.org/	Master directory of online resources used by news reporters (most are fee-based

	services)
OTHER LINKS PAGES	
Handy Terrific Links for Attorneys http://www.htla.org/HTLAlinks.html	The name says it all. This is the one page mega-list that covers the waterfront. A great start page for busy lawyers and executives.
Search Systems http://www.searchsystems.net/	Okay, I'm impressed. More than 8,800 free public data resources linked from this site, sensibly indexed both topically and geographically. Somebody deserves a medal for this one!
Attorney's Toolbox http://www.macattorney.com/tools.html	An interesting and useful hodge-podge of sites assembled by a California

	attorney
CEOExpress http://www.ceoexpress.com/	CEOExpress is comprehensive, quick and easy. A great resource!
Nations' Legal Links http://www.howardnations.com/nlli.html	Houston personal injury attorney Howard Nations maintains a well-organized and comprehensive links site of particular use to lawyers. His brain injury links are especially noteworthy.
Texas Almanac Links http://www.texasalmanac.com/links.html	The Texas Almanac offers a nice selection of links to Texas reference sources and agencies.
WashLaw WEB http://www.washlaw.edu/	This simple interface (by Washburn Univ.

	Law School) leads to a huge body of legal research resources.

I Have a Special Gift for My Readers

I appreciate my readers for without them I am just another struggling author attempting to make ends meet.

My readers and I have in common a passion for the written word as well as the desire to learn and grow from books.

My special offer to you is a massive ebook library that I have compiled over the years. It contains hundreds of fiction and non-fiction ebooks in Adobe Acrobat PDF format as well as the Greek classics and old literary classics too.

In fact, this library is so massive to completely download the entire library will require over 5 GBs open on your desktop.

Use the link below and scan all of the ebooks in the library. You can select the ebooks you want individually or download the entire library.

The link below does not expire after a given time period so you are free to return for more books rather than clog your desktop. And feel free to give the link to your friends who enjoy reading too.

I thank you for reading my book and hope if you are pleased that you will leave me an honest review so that I can improve my work and or write books that appeal to your interests.

Okay, here is the link…

http://tinyurl.com/special-readers-promo

PS: If you wish to reach me personally for any reason you may simply write to mailto:support@epubwealth.com.

I answer all of my emails so rest assured I will respond.

Meet the Author

Dr. Leland Benton is Director of Applied Web Info, a leading Internet Marketing company based in Utah with over 21,000 resellers in over 22-countries. Its operating entity – ePubWealth.com - is a leader in digital book publishing. He is also a behavioral scientist and Chief Forensics Investigator for ForensicsNation.com. Leland resides in Southern Utah.

Visit some of his websites
http://appliedmindsciences.com/
http://appliedwebinfo.com/
http://embarrassingproblemsfix.com/
http://www.epubwealth.com/
http://forensicsnation.com/
http://neternatives.com/
http://privacynations.com/
http://survivalnations.com/
http://thebentonkitchen.com
http://theolegions.org

www.ingramcontent.com/pod-product-compliance
Lightning Source LLC
Chambersburg PA
CBHW051733170526
45167CB00002B/916